MW00973239

Funding for this book was provided by

The State of Georgia
and
Gov. Zell Miller's
Reading Initiative
1998

Cobb County Public Library System

Capital Punishment

CRIME, JUSTICE, AND PUNISHMENT

Capital Punishment

Robert V. Wolf

Austin Sarat, GENERAL EDITOR

CHELSEA HOUSE PUBLISHERS
Philadelphia

Frontispiece: *The gas chamber at California's San Quentin Prison.*

Chelsea House Publishers

Production Manager Pamela Loos
Art Director Sara Davis
Picture Editor Judy Hasday
Senior Production Editor Lisa Chippendale

Staff for CAPITAL PUNISHMENT

Senior Editor John Ziff
Designer Takeshi Takahashi
Picture Researcher Patricia Burns
Cover Illustration Janet Hamlin

3 5 7 9 8 6 4 2

Library of Congress Cataloging-in-Publication Data

Wolf, Robert V.
Capital punishment / Robert V. Wolf; Austin Sarat, general editor.
     p. cm. — (Crime, justice, and punishment)
Includes index.
Summary: Surveys the history of the death penalty, describes different methods of execution, and discusses the legal and ethical ramifications using case histories.

ISBN 0-7910-4311-8

1. Capital punishment—United States—History—Juvenile literature. 2. Capital punishment—Moral and ethical aspects—United States—Juvenile literature. [1. Capital punishment.] I. Sarat, Austin. II. Title. III. Series
HV8699.U5W63 1997
364.66'0973—dc21   97-12035
                                                          CIP
                                                          AC

Contents

CRIME, JUSTICE, AND PUNISHMENT

Fears and Fascinations:

An Introduction to Crime, Justice, and Punishment

By Austin Sarat

We live with crime and images of crime all around us. Crime evokes in most of us a deep aversion, a feeling of profound vulnerability, but it also evokes an equally deep fascination. Today, in major American cities the fear of crime is a major fact of life, some would say a disproportionate response to the realities of crime. Yet the fear of crime is real, palpable in the quickened steps and furtive glances of people walking down darkened streets. At the same time, we eagerly follow crime stories on television and in movies. We watch with a "who done it" curiosity, eager to see the illicit deed done, the investigation undertaken, the miscreant brought to justice and given his just deserts. On the streets the presence of crime is a reminder of our own vulnerability and the precariousness of our taken-for-granted rights and freedoms. On television and in the movies the crime story gives us a chance to probe our own darker motives, to ask "Is there a criminal within?" as well as to feel the collective satisfaction of seeing justice done.

7

Fear and fascination, these two poles of our engagement with crime, are, of course, only part of the story. Crime is, after all, a major social and legal problem, not just an issue of our individual psychology. Politicians today use our fear of, and fascination with, crime for political advantage. How we respond to crime, as well as to the political uses of the crime issue, tells us a lot about who we are as a people as well as what we value and what we tolerate. Is our response compassionate or severe? Do we seek to understand or to punish, to enact an angry vengeance or to rehabilitate and welcome the criminal back into our midst? The CRIME, JUSTICE, AND PUNISHMENT series is designed to explore these themes, to ask why we are fearful and fascinated, to probe the meanings and motivations of crimes and criminals and of our responses to them, and, finally, to ask what we can learn about ourselves and the society in which we live by examining our responses to crime.

Crime is always a challenge to the prevailing normative order and a test of the values and commitments of law-abiding people. It is sometimes a Raskolnikov-like act of defiance, an assertion of the unwillingness of some to live according to the rules of conduct laid out by organized society. In this sense, crime marks the limits of the law and reminds us of law's all-too-regular failures. Yet sometimes there is more desperation than defiance in criminal acts; sometimes they signal a deep pathology or need in the criminal. To confront crime is thus also to come face-to-face with the reality of social difference, of class privilege and extreme deprivation, of race and racism, of children neglected, abandoned, or abused whose response is to enact on others what they have experienced themselves. And occasionally crime, or what is labeled a criminal act, represents a call for justice, an appeal to a higher moral order against the inadequacies of existing law.

Figuring out the meaning of crime and the motivations of criminals and whether crime arises from defiance, desperation, or the appeal for justice is never an easy task. The motivations and meanings of crime are as varied as are the persons who engage in criminal conduct. They are as mysterious as any of the mysteries of the human soul. Yet the desire to know the secrets of crime and the criminal is a strong one, for in that knowledge may lie one step on the road to protection, if not an assurance of one's own personal safety. Nonetheless, as strong as that desire may be, there is no available technology that can allow us to know the whys of crime with much confidence, let alone a scientific certainty. We can, however, capture something about crime by studying the defiance, desperation, and quest for justice that may be associated with it. Books in the CRIME, JUSTICE, AND PUNISHMENT series will take up that challenge. They tell stories of crime and criminals, some famous, most not, some glamorous and exciting, most mundane and commonplace.

This series will, in addition, take a sober look at American criminal justice, at the procedures through which we investigate crimes and identify criminals, at the institutions in which innocence or guilt is determined. In these procedures and institutions we confront the thrill of the chase as well as the challenge of protecting the rights of those who defy our laws. It is through the efficiency and dedication of law enforcement that we might capture the criminal; it is in the rare instances of their corruption or brutality that we feel perhaps our deepest betrayal. Police, prosecutors, defense lawyers, judges, and jurors administer criminal justice and in their daily actions give substance to the guarantees of the Bill of Rights. What is an adversarial system of justice? How does it work? Why do we have it? Books in the CRIME, JUSTICE, AND PUNISHMENT series will examine the thrill of the chase as we seek to capture the criminal. They will also reveal the drama and majesty of the criminal trial as well as the day-to-day reality of a criminal justice system in which trials are the exception and negotiated pleas of guilty are the rule.

When the trial is over or the plea has been entered, when we have separated the innocent from the guilty, the moment of punishment has arrived. The injunction to punish the guilty, to respond to pain inflicted by inflicting pain, is as old as civilization itself. "An eye for an eye and a tooth for a tooth" is a biblical reminder that punishment must measure pain for pain. But our response to the criminal must be better than and different from the crime itself. The biblical admonition, along with the constitutional prohibition of "cruel and unusual punishment," signals that we seek to punish justly and to be just not only in the determination of who can and should be punished, but in how we punish as well. But neither reminder tells us what to do with the wrongdoer. Do we rape the rapist, or burn the home of the arsonist? Surely justice and decency say no. But, if not, then how can and should we punish? In a world in which punishment is neither identical to the crime nor an automatic response to it, choices must be made and we must make them. Books in the CRIME, JUSTICE, AND PUNISHMENT series will examine those choices and the practices, and politics, of punishment. How do we punish and why do we punish as we do? What can we learn about the rationality and appropriateness of today's responses to crime by examining our past and its responses? What works? Is there, and can there be, a just measure of pain?

CRIME, JUSTICE, AND PUNISHMENT brings together books on some of the great themes of human social life. The books in this series capture our fear and fascination with crime and examine our responses to it. They remind us of the deadly seriousness of these subjects. They bring together themes in law, literature, and popular culture to challenge us to think again, to think anew, about subjects that go to the heart of who we are and how we can and will live together.

*   *   *   *   *

The death penalty is the law's most visible and dramatic criminal punishment. It expresses society's desire for vengeance and/or the belief that simple justice demands a life for a life. Because execution is irreversible, in the past the courts insisted on special legal procedures designed to ensure heightened reliability in capital cases. Yet recently our society has become impatient and frustrated with the slow pace at which death sentences lead to executions. The result has been a cutback in the procedural protections accorded to persons accused of a capital crime. This development is yet another in the anguished and complicated history of capital punishment in the United States, a history that will surely become even more anguished and complicated as we execute more and more people.

Capital Punishment provides a level-headed yet compelling account of that history and of the vexing legal issues surrounding the use of law's ultimate punishment. It reminds us that despite the current popularity of the death penalty, it has long been the subject of intense debate. Should the state have the right and power to kill any of its citizens? Can a state that refuses to avenge the loss of innocent life be worthy of our respect? By presenting stories of actual cases, this book reveals the human drama that lies behind these abstract questions and the struggles to find just responses to the gruesome deeds which lead to calls for capital punishment. It also provides an unusually lucid account of the legal and constitutional issues involved in the debate about the death penalty. Throughout, this book asks its readers to decide for themselves whether death as a punishment comports with our society's highest aspirations and its understanding of what justice and morality require.

Capital Punishment

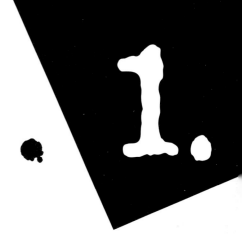

An American Tug-of-War

t 11:45 P.M. on March 19, 1995, prison officials escorted 32-year-old Thomas Grasso into a chamber deep in the heart of the Oklahoma State Penitentiary. He chatted with those in attendance as a guard strapped him to a gurney. Once he was tied down, an attendant stuck a needle, which was attached to tubes that extended through a hole in the wall, into Grasso's arm. The prison warden then addressed the gallery of witnesses, among whom were Grasso's two lawyers and 12 reporters. "Mr. Grasso is not going to make any statements," the warden announced, "so we will begin the execution."

On the other side of the chamber wall, three exe-

Convicted killer Thomas Grasso (center) is led into court. Sentenced to 20 years to life for a murder he committed in New York and to death for a murder he committed in Oklahoma, Grasso was at the center of a legal struggle between the governors of the two states, who stood at opposite ends of the death penalty issue.

cutioners, whose identities were concealed by hoods and who had been paid $300 apiece for their work, began to feed chemicals into the intravenous tubes: sodium thiopental, which caused Grasso to pass out; pancuronium bromide, which froze Grasso's lungs; and potassium chloride, which stopped Grasso's heart. After five minutes, a doctor lifted the lid over Grasso's left eye and felt for his pulse. He then turned to those assembled and announced that Grasso had died at 12:22 A.M.

Grasso had admitted to brutally murdering two elderly people over a six-month period in two different states. His first victim was Hilda Johnson, 87, of Tulsa, Oklahoma. He had entered her house on December 24, 1990, under the pretense of offering her a Christmas gift. He then beat her with a piece of wood and an electric iron and strangled her to death with a cord of Christmas lights. He escaped with $12 and a television set. His second victim was a neighbor of his, 81-year-old Leslie Holtz. Grasso robbed and strangled Holtz on July 3, 1991, in a boardinghouse in New York City.

Because the crimes occurred in two states, Grasso was put on trial in both New York, which did not have the death penalty, and Oklahoma, which did. The New York court sentenced him to 20 years to life for killing Holtz. The Oklahoma court sentenced him to death for the murder of Johnson.

The question then arose: Who would get to punish Grasso first? New York governor Mario Cuomo, who opposed the death penalty, wanted Grasso to serve his 20 years first. Oklahoma governor David L. Waters, who supported the death penalty, wanted Grasso executed as soon as possible. Waters felt that keeping Grasso alive another 20 years was a waste of time and money.

People in both states took sides on the issue. On one side were those who favored immediate execution, such as a man who owned a delicatessen in which both

Grasso and Holtz used to shop. "This guy's a cold-blooded murderer as far as I'm concerned. [By being executed,] he's getting what he deserves," the deli owner told the *Staten Island Advance*, a local newspaper.

On the other side were people like the Reverend Don Brooks, who led a protest outside the prison gate during the execution. "We oppose the taking of human life, whether it's by Grasso or the state of Oklahoma. We can't stop killing by killing," Brooks said.

In the end, a judge agreed that New York had the right to keep Grasso for 20 years because it had convicted him first. Cuomo considered this a victory, but it was short lived. In the 1994 election, his opponent, George Pataki, made Cuomo's opposition to the death penalty a major issue. He said Cuomo coddled murderers and was soft on crime. In the end, Cuomo lost the election.

Former New York governor Mario Cuomo (center) at a rally against the death penalty outside the state capitol building in Albany. Cuomo's outspoken opposition to capital punishment, and his refusal to turn over Thomas Grasso to Oklahoma to be executed, contributed to his 1994 election loss to George Pataki. Soon after taking office, Pataki sent Grasso to Oklahoma and restored New York's death penalty.

Within a few days of taking office, Pataki put Grasso on a plane to Oklahoma, where he was executed. A few months later, Pataki signed a bill making the death penalty legal in New York for the first time in 30 years.

The Grasso debate struck at the core of how America feels about the death penalty, the most severe punishment in the arsenal of the criminal justice system. It's a debate that has been raging for more than a century, and one whose resolution seems to be nowhere in sight.

States like New York, which banned capital punishment in 1965 only to reinstate it 30 years later, have frequently gone back and forth on the issue. From 1897 to 1917, for instance, 10 states repealed the death penalty; but within only a few years, 8 states had reinstated it. Another dramatic example of a change of heart is Delaware: in 1958 it got rid of the death penalty, but in 1961 it brought capital punishment back. At the beginning of 1996, 38 states had death penalty statutes and more were considering them.

The Supreme Court, too, has taken varying approaches to the issue. For centuries the Court never questioned the constitutionality of the death penalty. Then in 1972, it declared that every death penalty law in the nation violated the Constitution's Eighth Amendment ban on cruel and unusual punishment. Four years later the Supreme Court okayed new death penalty laws.

Since then the number of executions has been slowly on the rise, increasing to 56 executions in 1995. Fifty-six may not sound like a lot, but that number represents an 80 percent rise over the previous year and a fourfold increase from 1991. It is also the most people executed in a single year in the United States since

ON THE RETURN OF THE DEATH PENALTY TO NEW YORK

When a society does not express its own horror at the crime of murder by enforcing the ultimate sanction against it, innocent lives are put at risk.

This bill is going to save lives.

—George E. Pataki, governor of New York

This is a step back in what should be a march constantly toward a higher level of civility and intelligence. The argument that the death penalty will deter and reduce crimes has been abandoned almost everywhere.

—Mario M. Cuomo, former governor of New York

1960. Watt Espy, a capital punishment historian, said in a 1995 interview that he expects the United States will soon break the single-year record of 199 executions, set in 1935.

To get an idea of how and why the death penalty is administered in the United States today—as well as to understand what Americans think about capital punishment—it is necessary to examine the history of this most severe of punishments. It is a history that spans thousands of years and countless societies.

A LONG HISTORY

lmost every culture throughout history has relied on capital punishment and justified it as a necessary tool for exacting retribution or maintaining order. The only things that changed over the course of time were the crimes deemed punishable by death and the methods used to kill those found guilty.

To modern sensibilities, some of the ancient laws seem barbaric. For instance, in ancient Persia, one method of execution involved being eaten alive by insects and vermin. In the Middle Ages, methods of execution included chopping off arms and legs, impaling on a stake, stripping off the condemned person's skin, boiling in oil, drawing and quartering (cutting out a person's entrails and then tearing his body into four pieces), burning at the stake, and crucifixion.

The Bible authorizes executing those who show contempt for their parents, walk without permission on sacred ground, practice sorcery, sacrifice to foreign gods,

Executions used to be public spectacles, as this 1936 photograph attests. About 20,000 people gathered in Owensboro, Kentucky, on the morning of August 14 to see the hanging of a 22-year-old black man, Rainey Bethea.

This 17th-century drawing depicts a man being quartered—torn into four pieces by horses. Quartering was a popular method of execution in Europe.

or prostitute themselves, among other transgressions. Citing the Bible, colonial Americans made witchcraft, idolatry, and stubbornness in a child capital crimes. Even today, some people defend capital punishment by quoting a passage in Exodus that says, "you shall give life for life, eye for eye, tooth for tooth, hand for hand, foot for foot, burn for burn, wound for wound, stroke for stroke." (Bible scholars point out, however, that ancient judges in actual practice rarely issued death edicts. And opponents of the death penalty note that other sections of the Bible advocate mercy and forgiveness.)

One of the stranger capital crimes was laid out by Henry VIII, who ruled England from 1509 to 1547. He prescribed the death penalty for anyone who imagined the death of the king. England was also the site of one of the darkest episodes in the history of capital punishment when, during the 18th century, the number of capital crimes ballooned to well over 300. The list was so long that it became known as the "Bloody Code." People were executed for, among other things, stealing

as little as five shillings, forgery, consorting with Gyp-
sies, and pickpocketing. Because so many crimes were
punishable by death, executions—usually by hanging—
were frequent. They were actually festive occasions,
and vendors sold refreshments to the hundreds and
sometimes thousands of people who came to watch.

In colonial America, and even after the Revolu-
tionary War, executions were extravagant public affairs
and often included a procession from the prison to the
gallows and a lengthy sermon by a minister. It was felt
that executions reflected "God's law" and were necessary for maintaining order. Typically, the minister
speaking at an execution warned the assembled crowd
that the same thing could happen to them if they didn't
abide by the law. At the execution of Moses Dunbar in
1777 for treason, pastor Nathan Strong exhorted:

> People are not far from destruction who disobey the pub-
> lic acts of their own government—who endeavor artfully
> to elude the institutions of their own legislature—who
> think themselves better judges of safety, and the means of
> preservation than the collected wisdom of the whole. . . .
> Let such persons . . . be warned by the proceedings of this
> day and do no more so wickedly.

Hanging was the most common method of execution in the United States at that time. Until the 19th
century, hanging consisted of tying a knotted rope
around the condemned person's neck and pushing him
off a ladder or platform, whereupon the condemned
would slowly strangle to death. Later, the "drop" was
invented whereby the offender was dropped through a
trap door. If properly done, the body dropped with suf-
ficient force that the condemned person's neck broke
instantly. But other methods were used as well. Slave
women convicted of crimes were often burned to death.
After a slave revolt in 1812 in Louisiana, 16 slaves were
decapitated in a town square and their heads were
placed on pikes along the Mississippi River as a warning to other slaves. During the Salem witch trials in

1692, a man who refused to testify after his wife was accused of witchcraft was "pressed" to death; the sentence was carried out by laying him on a stone floor, placing a board over him, and piling stones upon the board. Historians believe the man, Giles Corey, was between 80 and 90 years old.

In France, the method of execution was intended to match the crime and the convict's social rank. Those of high rank, such as noblemen, were afforded the most refined death—beheading by sword. Although such a death could be messy, especially if more than one blow was required, it was surely less painful than methods reserved for people of lower rank. People of lower rank convicted of counterfeiting faced being boiled alive, heretics were burned, and highway robbers were often beaten to death.

Over the last 200 years, execution methods have changed as society has sought to make the process more "civilized." That was the wish of Dr. Joseph Ignace Guillotin when, in 1789, he strongly advocated use of a killing machine invented by Antoine Louis, a French physician, that he thought would do the job quickly and painlessly. The device, dubbed the guillotine, used a large blade to chop off the head of the condemned and remained the standard method of execution in France until capital punishment was abolished in 1981. A similar motivation caused Dr. Alfred Porter Southwick, a resident of New York, to pronounce almost a hundred years after Guillotin: "Science and civilization demand some more humane method than the rope. The rope is a relic of barbarism."

Southwick, a member of a New York State commission on capital punishment, directed his comments to the inventor Thomas Alva Edison, who, at Southwick's

FROM THE BIBLE

Whoever strikes a man a mortal blow must be put to death.

—Exodus 21:12

"Be compassionate, as your Father is compassionate. Do not judge, and you will not be judged. Do not condemn, and you will not be condemned. Pardon, and you shall be pardoned."

—Luke 6:36-38

Nearly every culture throughout history has practiced capital punishment. In India, executions were sometimes carried out by having an elephant crush the condemned's head.

request, invented a thoroughly modern method of execution: death by electrocution. The condemned person was strapped into a chair, electrodes were placed on his head and his spine, and then a massive dose of electric current was applied for about 20 seconds. People suggested various names for Edison's invention, including "ampermort," "dynamort," and "electricide." The name that finally stuck was electric chair.

Benjamin Rush, credited with beginning the movement to abolish capital punishment in the United States, declared in 1792 that reform, not retribution, should be the goal of punishment.

It was first used on August 6, 1890, to execute William Kemmler, a Buffalo, New York, fruit peddler convicted of murdering his girlfriend with an axe. After a 17-second jolt of electricity, Kemmler appeared dead. But then he stirred slightly. Immediately, the current was turned back on. Kemmler groaned and jerked about, causing witnesses to vomit and faint. Even the district attorney who had prosecuted Kemmler fled in disgust.

Despite its bungled premiere, politicians and the public came to believe that the chair was more efficient than hanging and that it lessened the suffering of the executed. The electric chair eventually became the most popular method of execution in the United States, with 26 states using it by 1951. But soon new methods came along, and in many states the electric chair was replaced. Currently only 11 states use the chair. In New York, where the electric chair was invented, it was used to kill 695 people before the state abolished the death penalty in 1965. (New York's recently reinstated death penalty law provides for death by lethal injection.)

The gas chamber came along in 1924. It was invented by D. A. Turner, a major in the U.S. Army Medical Corps, who thought the gas chamber less cruel than the electric chair. The gas chamber is currently used as an option in only seven states. The chamber itself is octagonal in shape. The condemned person is strapped into a chair, and a stethoscope is strapped to his chest and connected to earpieces in a witness room so that a doctor can note when the heart stops beating. Under the convict's chair is a bowl, and above the bowl cyanide is suspended. An executioner releases sulfuric acid through a tube into the bowl and then drops the cyanide into the acid. A chemical reaction occurs, releasing cyanide gas. The gas eventually kills the convict by paralyzing the heart and lungs, but the process can take up to 12 minutes.

Lethal injection is now the most popular method of execution in the United States, and it, too, was devised as a more humane method of killing. It was first used in Oklahoma in 1977 and is currently the sole method or an option in 32 states. But it has had problems as well. In Texas in 1988, for instance, the tube carrying the poisons into Raymond Landry began to leak, spraying witnesses with the deadly chemicals. Landry was half-dead when the tubes were reinserted, and it took him 24 minutes to die.

ON HUMANE METHODS OF EXECUTION

My machine will take off a head in a twinkling, and the victim will feel nothing but a slight sense of refreshing coolness on the neck. We cannot make too much haste, gentlemen, to allow the nation to enjoy this advantage.

—**Joseph Ignace Guillotin, 18th-century French proponent of the guillotine**

Science and civilization demand some more humane method than the rope. The rope is a relic of barbarism.

—**Alfred Porter Southwick, 19th-century advocate of death by electrocution**

Being a former farmer and horse raiser, I know what it's like to try to eliminate an injured horse by shooting him. Now you call the veterinarian and the vet gives it a shot and the horse goes to sleep—that's it.

—**Ronald Reagan, 40th president of the United States, on lethal injection**

Some of the more traditional execution methods are still on the books. As of 1996, hanging remained an option in Delaware, Montana, New Hampshire, and Washington, while Idaho and Utah still allowed death by firing squad.

The death penalty has seen perhaps its greatest use during wars and revolutions. This occurred, for example, during the French Revolution, when the newly invented guillotine became a mass killing machine. It's not known exactly how many people were executed by the revolutionaries, but estimates range from 17,000 to 40,000. Among those killed were Queen Marie Antoinette and King Louis XVI.

In the United States, people of lower social and economic rank have generally faced execution more often than people who are rich or of high social standing. As shall be discussed later, one of the major criticisms of capital punishment in the United States is that members of minority groups, who often have less economic resources and thus usually can't afford the best possible defense, have been disproportionately affected by the death penalty. Even in the earliest days of the Republic, those most often sentenced to die were "outsiders"—foreigners, minorities, and people not from the immediate community—says death penalty historian Louis Mesier. "Juries most likely found it easier to convict outsiders . . . of capital crimes, and governors felt less pressure to commute the death sentence of those with few ties to the community," Mesier writes. Watt Espy, another death penalty historian, maintains that capital punishment has been used "almost genocidally against blacks," a pattern, he says, that began during the time of slavery and has continued into the present.

Throughout American history, voices have been raised against capital punishment. Among the first were the Quakers, who were philosophically opposed to the death penalty and whose laws in South Jersey in the 17th century did not provide for it. Later, however, the

British monarch made the colonies adopt severe penal laws, and it wasn't until after the American Revolution that a significant, organized opposition to the death penalty first got a solid foothold. The man credited with founding that movement was Dr. Benjamin Rush, a Philadelphia physician and signer of the Declaration of Independence.

Rush was a prolific writer and innovator who expressed his views on countless subjects—he attacked slavery, called for public health reforms, and helped found the science of psychiatry, among numerous other causes. When it came to capital punishment, he was strongly influenced by the Enlightenment in Europe in the mid-1700s and was particularly moved by the ideas of the Italian legal scholar Cesare Beccaria.

Beccaria argued in a famous essay, "On Crimes and Punishments," that an execution failed in one of its primary goals—to deter people from committing more crimes. Instead of instilling fear in observers, he said, it merely made people feel sorry for the convict. The "momentary spectacle" of an execution was also too brief to have a lasting impact on society, Beccaria claimed. Instead, Beccaria said, lengthy imprisonment—which was a new idea at the time—would be a more effective alternative. Not only would it curb future crimes "by the long and painful example of a man deprived of liberty," but the guilty party would pay back the community "with his labors."

Around the same time, penitentiaries were being built. They differed from jails in that they isolated a prisoner from other inmates. In 1792 Rush wrote that life imprisonment in a penitentiary was better than execution because it left open the possibility of rehabilitation. Underlying this was the new idea that people weren't born criminals; rather, it was believed, social influences turned people into criminals. Thus, Rush maintained, reform, as opposed to retribution, should motivate punishment.

In addition, Rush argued that killing a convicted criminal makes society more used to murder and thus lessens the horror of it. To Rush, the death penalty was a remnant of monarchies, when kings had the power to kill their subjects at will. This, he said, was offensive to the "mild and benevolent" principles of the new republican government.

A friend of Rush's, William Bradford, who eventually became attorney general of the United States, became a partial supporter of Rush's cause. Bradford didn't oppose capital punishment outright, but he argued that capital crimes should be more limited in scope. He suggested, for instance, that not all homicides be capital crimes. Instead, he pressed for separate categories of murder: first degree, which meant killing that was intentional and thus punishable by death; and second

In modern times, societies have sought to make executions more "humane." Such was the goal of the guillotine (below), which severed the condemned's head with a heavy blade, and the electric chair (opposite page), which kills with a massive dose of electrical current.

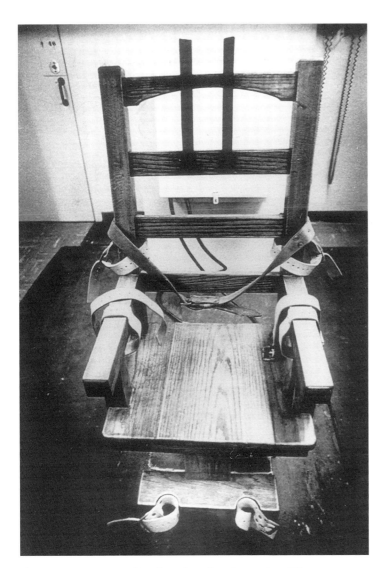

degree, to cover all other kinds of murder. This proposal was adopted in Pennsylvania and Virginia in 1794.

Those who opposed capital punishment made further headway a few years later when Pennsylvania and Kentucky dropped the death penalty for all crimes except murder.

But many parts of the United States remained avowedly loyal to the death penalty, and the high-minded arguments of abolitionists had little or no effect. Often, it remained a local issue, carried out by sheriffs in local squares. For them, hanging a suspected or convicted criminal was a matter of convenience, because they lacked facilities for long-term incarceration and it was difficult to transport prisoners possibly hundreds of miles to more secure state institutions.

Rush died in 1813, but he left a powerful legacy. Organizations to fight the death penalty were formed, and by the 1830s and 1840s, the anti-death-penalty movement began to have a significant impact. More states began reducing the number of capital crimes and making laws more flexible. By 1846 in Michigan, treason was the only capital crime. In 1852 Rhode Island eliminated capital punishment for everything except murder committed by a convict already sentenced to life in prison. By 1861 three-quarters of the states had removed burglary and robbery from their lists of capital crimes. By the turn of the century 18 states and U.S. territories allowed juries, at their discretion, to grant life imprisonment for capital crimes.

In 1837 Maine adopted a law that subsequent governors interpreted to mean that the courts could issue death sentences but that the governor couldn't enforce them. In 1853 Wisconsin eliminated capital punishment entirely, and from 1897 to 1917 a total of 10 more states followed suit. Motivation for abolishing the death penalty varied. In Minnesota in 1906, for instance, a man was hanged with a rope that was too long; instead of dying instantly from a broken neck, the man dangled in the air for more than 14 minutes until he died by strangulation. So many people were disgusted by the bungled execution that it led to the 1911 repeal of Minnesota's death penalty laws.

Yet when it comes to the death penalty, Americans have never been able to reach a lasting consensus. Some people in the states where capital punishment no longer existed took the law into their own hands, dragging suspected criminals from their houses and jails and killing them. This kind of vigilante activity, in which criminals or suspects are killed outside the law, is called "lynching," and historically blacks—particularly in the South—have been frequent victims. In part to reduce the number of lynchings, 8 of the 10 states that had abolished the death penalty from 1897 to 1917 reinstated it within a few years.

Not until 1957 would another state—Delaware—repeal the death penalty. But by then, anti-death-penalty advocates had begun to change their methods. Rather than lobbying on a state-by-state basis, they decided to fight it out in the courts. They had observed that the Supreme Court by the mid-20th century had shown a willingness to apply the Constitution to states in a myriad of issues, from ordering the desegregation of schools to the elimination of tests at voting booths. They hoped that, given the right case, the Supreme Court would take a stand on the death penalty as well, either limiting its scope or, in a move considered a long shot by most people, banning the death penalty altogether by declaring it unconstitutional.

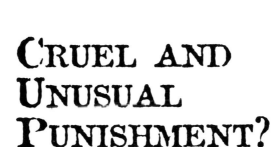

CRUEL AND UNUSUAL PUNISHMENT?

he Constitution of the United States guarantees to every citizen certain fundamental rights. The First Amendment, for example, guarantees freedom of religion, speech, press, assembly, and petition. The Second Amendment promises that "the right of the people to keep and bear arms shall not be infringed." The amendment most relevant to the issue of the death penalty is the Eighth Amendment. It reads:

> Excessive bail shall not be required, nor excessive fines imposed, nor cruel and unusual punishment inflicted.

However simple and straightforward these words may sound, it's not always clear what they mean. That's

A march against the death penalty in Columbia, South Carolina. By the late 1960s opponents of capital punishment had begun to change their tactics from lobbying individual state legislatures to focusing on constitutional challenges that might end the death penalty nationwide.

because the words *cruel* and *unusual* are subjective. One person may think, for instance, that capital punishment is cruel and unusual, while another person may not. Or a person may think that execution by lethal injection isn't cruel and unusual but that execution by firing squad is.

It is the job of the courts to help interpret such words as "cruel and unusual." In fact, every law in the country is open to interpretation, and the courts play a vital role in establishing their meaning. The court that gets the final say is the Supreme Court, which has nine judges, or justices, and is the most powerful court in the land.

By the 1960s opponents of capital punishment hoped to get a case before the Supreme Court so they could argue that the death penalty was cruel and unusual. They were encouraged in 1963 by an opinion written by Justice Arthur Goldberg. In the opinion, Goldberg suggested that the death penalty for rape might be unconstitutional. Death penalty opponents believed this was a sign that the Court could be convinced to slow, reduce, or stop altogether the use of the death penalty.

In an attempt to speed this development, lawyers representing death-row inmates began appealing more and more cases to the Supreme Court. The Court, however, took no immediate action on these cases. From 1967 to 1972, hundreds of cases piled up. Without a Supreme Court decision, the executions couldn't take place. Thus, by not acting, the Court instituted an unofficial moratorium on executions. Opponents of the death penalty were thrilled, even though they knew that eventually the Court would act, and possibly the executions would begin again. Still, they hoped that when the Supreme Court finally responded to the appeals, it would determine that capital punishment violated the Eighth Amendment and was therefore unconstitutional.

Leading the fight against the death penalty was the Legal Defense Fund of the National Association for the Advancement of Colored People (NAACP). The Legal Defense Fund opposed capital punishment primarily because it felt that the death penalty was applied in a racist manner, especially in the South, where most executions took place. Since 1930, for instance, more than half of the people executed in America had been black, even though blacks committed much fewer than half of the crimes. Also, a black man convicted of raping a white woman had a much higher likelihood of being executed than a black man convicted of raping a

Twelve proposed amendments to the U.S. Constitution, passed by Congress on March 4, 1789. The states failed to ratify the first 2, but the remaining 10 became the Bill of Rights. Did the death penalty violate the Eighth Amendment's ban on "cruel and unusual punishment"? The course of capital punishment in America would turn on this crucial question.

Law professor Anthony Amsterdam (at right) argued against capital punishment before the Supreme Court in the Furman v. Georgia *case. Among other points, Amsterdam said that the death penalty was randomly applied.*

black woman or a white man convicted of raping either a black or a white woman. Often, too, blacks were tried by a white judge before all-white juries, and with the long history of racial discrimination in the South, it hardly seemed likely that their views weren't clouded by some form of prejudice.

The Legal Defense Fund used a number of cases to bring these and other arguments against the death penalty before the Supreme Court. One such case was

McGautha v. California, in which the Court considered the appeal of Dennis McGautha, who had been convicted of committing a murder during an armed robbery. A jury had sentenced him to death, but Legal Defense Fund attorneys argued that the jury had too much freedom in determining punishment. Without explicit guidelines, a jury could hand down a death sentence based on whim and caprice, which violated the "due process" clause of the Fourteenth Amendment, McGautha's attorneys argued.

But the Supreme Court, in a 6-3 decision in 1971, rejected the Legal Defense Fund's arguments, finding that it would be impossible to write guidelines describing "those characteristics of criminal homicides and their perpetrators which call for the death penalty" in a way that was fair, complete, and comprehensible to everyone. The Court further said that guidelines were unnecessary because juries, "confronted with the truly awesome responsibility of decreeing death for a fellow human," would take the job seriously and not act on whim.

Interestingly, just a year later, the Court was to reverse itself in a case that caused a historic shift in the way the death penalty was viewed. The facts of the case were these: At 2:00 in the morning on August 11, 1967, William Henry Furman—a black man—shot to death William Micki, a 29-year-old white who served in the Coast Guard. Furman broke into Micki's home in Savannah, Georgia, to steal a television set, but Micki caught him in the act. As he was fleeing, Furman's gun went off—he told his lawyer later that he tripped on an electric cord and the gun fired accidentally. The bullet passed through a closed door and entered Micki's upper chest, killing him within five minutes.

Furman's trial took only one day. In the morning the jury—11 whites and 1 black—was selected. Nine witnesses spoke on behalf of the prosecution. The only person to speak for the defense was Furman himself. He declared that the shooting had been accidental. But almost as important was what the jury didn't hear: that psychiatrists found that Furman had a "mental deficiency" and suffered from "psychotic episodes." By 5:10 in the afternoon, the jury had reached its verdict: guilty. As for sentencing, the jury had to choose between mercy, which meant life imprisonment, or no mercy, which meant the electric chair. The jury chose no mercy.

Furman's attorney, B. Clarence Mayfield, appealed the decision. The Georgia Supreme Court upheld the verdict, so Mayfield, with the help of the Legal Defense Fund, appealed to the Supreme Court. The case languished there for several years, but finally, in 1971, the Supreme Court announced it had decided to hear Furman's case along with three others from the hundreds of death-row cases before it. The Court even announced that it was interested in only a single issue: Was the death penalty "cruel and unusual punishment"?

The hearing took place on January 17, 1972. In arguing before the Court, Legal Defense Fund attorney Anthony Amsterdam attacked the death penalty on several major points. He said capital punishment violated society's current "standards of decency." He also said that capital punishment was applied randomly. There were people sentenced to die for armed robbery, he said, while others who had committed the far-worse crime of murder were facing only life in prison. In fact, had the

In the Supreme Court's landmark 1972 Furman decision, Justice Thurgood Marshall (at left) joined Justice William Brennan in declaring the death penalty cruel and unusual—and therefore unconstitutional—under any circumstances. The other three justices who joined Marshall and Brennan in the 5-4 majority were less definitive, implying that death penalty laws as they were currently written were unconstitutional.

jurors in Furman's case heard that he had a mental deficiency, they might have been more lenient. That made no sense, Amsterdam said, and thus the entire process of choosing who would die was unfair.

The Court was also presented with statistical evidence that the death penalty had been used mainly against poor people and minorities. For example, a man convicted of raping a white woman, if he was black, had a 38 percent chance of getting the death penalty, but if he was white, there was only a half a percent likelihood.

Arguing in favor of capital punishment were states with the death penalty. Among the states' arguments was the claim that the Court had no right to interfere in the implementation of capital punishment; that right, it was argued, belonged only to state legislatures, which were elected by the people. It was also argued that execution by itself wasn't cruel and that as long as the execution was performed in a humane way, it conformed with the Eighth Amendment.

The justices spent months mulling the case, which became known as *Furman v. Georgia*. Finally, on June 29, 1972, the Court issued nine separate opinions—one written by each justice—making it one of the longest decisions in the Supreme Court's history.

Ultimately, five of the justices—the slimmest possible majority—accepted at least some of the arguments against the death penalty. Two justices, William Brennan and Thurgood Marshall, accepted all of the arguments, agreeing that the death penalty was cruel and unusual and therefore unconstitutional. None of the other justices, however, stood so solidly against the death penalty. Instead, they accepted various facets of the anti-death-penalty arguments, essentially stating that the death penalty laws as they were written were unfair.

Some of the justices were persuaded to believe that the death penalty was arbitrary, and they pointed out that most states had no guidelines for when capital punishment was appropriate; that left judges and juries with unlimited discretion, they said. "The death sentences are cruel and unusual in the same way that being struck by lightning is cruel and unusual. . . . [T]he [Eighth Amendment] cannot tolerate the infliction of a sentence of death under legal systems that permit this unique penalty to be so wantonly and freakishly imposed," wrote Justice Potter Stewart.

The effect of the 5-4 decision was stunning. All the death penalty laws in the 32 states that allowed capital punishment were unconstitutional, and the death sentences of the 629 convicts currently on death row were automatically overturned. The United States was effectively without a death penalty, and the justices hadn't clearly stated whether or not new death penalty laws, if written differently, would be acceptable. Some of the justices indicated, however, that sentencing guidelines governing judges and juries might make the process more fair. This gave legislatures around the country a sketchy blueprint for reinstating the death penalty, and many of them began almost immediately writing new laws that they hoped would pass constitutional muster.

THE RETURN
OF THE DEATH
PENALTY

Although the Supreme Court sanctioned new death penalty statutes in 1976, that by no means settled the issue of public opinion. Here a death penalty opponent makes his views known in front of the Supreme Court. There is an irony here: the man pictured on the sign, Gary Gilmore, wanted to be executed. He eventually got his wish, dying by firing squad in Utah.

After the *Furman* decision, 35 states rushed to pass new death penalty statutes. Typical of the new laws was Georgia's, which called for a two-part trial: first the jury judges guilt, and then, if the defendant is found guilty, the jury decides whether or not to impose the death penalty. In determining punishment, the jury must consider mitigating and aggravating circumstances. A mitigating circumstance might be the defendant's youth or the fact that he cooperated with police; an aggravating circumstance might be the fact that the defendant has a long criminal history or that the crime was committed for money. The Georgia law also required that all death sentences be automatically appealed to the state supreme court.

Many states passed similar laws with slight variations. In Florida, for example, the jury was given guidelines, including aggravating and mitigating circumstances, but its decision was only advisory. The judge had the final say in sentencing and retained the power to override the jury's recommendation. Texas, in place of guidelines, required the jury to answer three questions in a hearing that would take place following a guilty verdict in a capital murder trial. The three questions were: whether the defendant's actions had been deliberate and likely to result in death; whether the defendant's conduct had been "unreasonable to the provocation, if any, by the deceased"; and whether there existed a "probability" the defendant would commit further violent acts that would threaten society.

And some states, such as North Carolina and Louisiana, took a different approach entirely. Rather than issue guidelines, those states decided to make capital punishment mandatory for certain kinds of murder, such as first-degree murder.

In reviewing these new laws in 1976, the U.S. Supreme Court looked favorably on the statutes that gave juries guidance in making their decisions, including the laws passed by Georgia (*Gregg v. Georgia*), Florida (*Proffitt v. Florida*), and Texas (*Jurek v. Texas*). "These procedures require the jury to consider the circumstances of the crime and the criminal before it recommends sentence. No longer can a Georgia jury do what Furman's jury did: Reach a finding of the defendant's guilt and then, without guidance or direction, decide whether he should live or die," wrote Justice Potter Stewart.

However, the Court, in a 5-4 decision, rejected mandatory sentencing, such as had been adopted in North Carolina (*Woodson v. North Carolina*) and Louisiana (*Roberts v. Louisiana*). The main problem with such statutes, the justices found, was that they didn't allow judges or juries to consider an individual's unique culpability and circumstance, instead treating

ON REHABILITATION

The reformation of offenders . . . is not effected at all by capital punishments, which exterminate instead of reforming, and should be the last melancholy resource against those whose existence is become inconsistent with the safety of their fellow citizens. . . .

**—Thomas Jefferson,
third president of the United States**

It is my personal belief that if [they're] not rehabilitated after 15 years [in the criminal justice system], kill 'em.

—Tim Jennings, New Mexico state senator

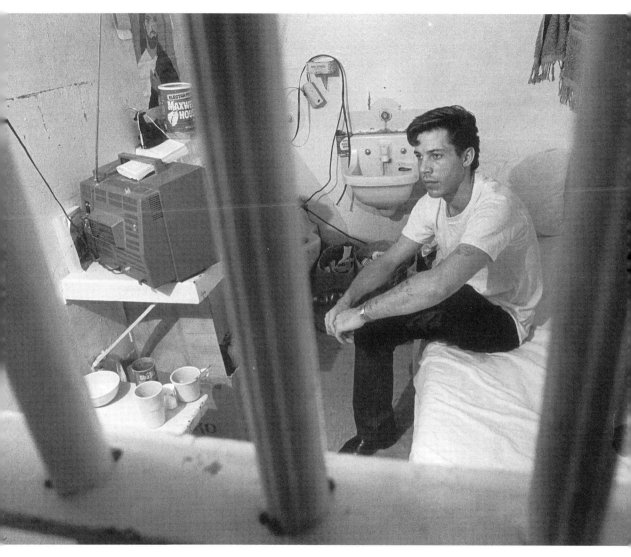

all those convicted of first-degree murder "as members of a faceless, undifferentiated mass to be subjected to the blind infliction of the penalty of death," Justice Stewart wrote in the *Woodson* decision.

It didn't take long for the number of convicts on death row to surpass the pre-*Furman* number of 629. By 1981 there were 794 people on death row; by 1985 there were nearly 1,500 people condemned to die, and by 1995 the number had surpassed 3,000.

A death-row inmate sits in his six-by-eight-foot cell—where he spends 23 hours of each day—inside the Louisiana State Prison in Angola. On average, condemned prisoners wait eight years before their sentence is carried out.

Interestingly, however, the number of actual executions has remained relatively low. In 1981, for instance, only one person was executed. By the mid-1980s, only about 1 percent of those on death row were actually executed, a figure that remained fairly steady through 1994, when only 31 people out of almost 3,000 condemned prisoners were actually put to death. The figure rose closer to 2 percent, however, in 1995, when 56 people out of 3,100 on death row were executed.

Overall, since 1976, about 5,000 people in the United States have been sentenced to die, more than 2,000 verdicts have been set aside, and 336 executions (as of May 1996) have been carried out. In October of 1995, Texas became the first state to have carried out 100 executions since 1976. Florida at the time had executed 34 people, the nation's second-highest total. Four states—Louisiana, Virginia, Texas, and Florida—have been responsible for two-thirds of the executions since 1976.

After receiving a death sentence, a convict typically waits on death row for years before the sentence is actually carried out. By 1995 the longest a person had been on death row since 1976 was more than 16 years, while the shortest time was a year and a half. The reason it takes so long to carry out a death sentence is that every prisoner is entitled to legal appeals, which can take years to make their way through the courts. In many cases, only after one appeal has been denied will a death-row prisoner file another appeal on another issue. Proponents of swifter punishment argue that this is one of the ways death-row prisoners manipulate the system, and there is considerable support for changing the laws

ON RETRIBUTION

The state continues to kill its victims, not so much to defend society against them—for it could do that equally well by imprisonment—but to appease the mob's emotions of hatred and revenge.

—Clarence Darrow, American lawyer

It used to be that the public generally thought the death penalty was a deterrent to crime. Now favoring it is more of a retribution argument, a life for a life. What is spurring this is the perception that crime is out of control and people want something done.

—Richard Dieter, executive director, Death Penalty Information Center

There are certain crimes that are so heinous, so egregious, so violent that your soul calls out for punishment of death.

—Edward I. Koch, former mayor of New York City

to restrict a prisoner's right to appeal. But advocates for death-row inmates insist that the time-consuming appeals process is essential to help correct trial errors and prevent the execution of an innocent person, a horrifying prospect that some people feel is not that improbable.

CAPITAL PUNISHMENT IN THE POST-*FURMAN* ERA: THE CASE OF JOHN SPENKELINK

Circuit judge John Rudd listens to an appeal by attorney Andrew Graham for a stay of execution for convicted murderer John Spenkelink, August 13, 1977. Rudd, who had originally sentenced Spenkelink to death in 1973, denied the appeal, but it would be almost two more years before Spenkelink faced the electric chair.

Debates about the constitutional meaning of cruel and unusual punishment, the length of the appeals process, and the composition of America's death-row population can all take on a mind-numbing, theoretical quality. But behind each argument and legal decision and statistic there is a very real man or woman, convicted of a real crime, whose fate hangs in the balance. Death or life. That is what it ultimately boils down to for those on death row.

One way to get a sense of how the death penalty operates in the post-*Furman* era is to look at one man's case. The following is the story of John Spenkelink, a convicted murderer, who was only the second person to be executed following the Supreme Court's 1976 decision.

John Arthur Spenkelink spent the last days of his life on "death watch." This is the term used to describe the final weeks leading up to a prisoner's execution. In Florida, where Spenkelink was jailed, it involves bringing the prisoner to a special small cell near the execution chamber, where the electric chair is located. The cell is just a little bigger than an average closet. This is how another Florida prisoner on death row described the death watch:

> You are in a cell that is located about thirty feet from the chair. You stay in that cell an average of twenty-three days. There are two ways out of that cell. One if you receive a stay of execution. The other is take that thirty-foot walk.

Spenkelink was on death row because he'd killed a man. The victim was Joseph J. Szymankiewicz. Spenkelink, who was 24 years old at the time, had met Szymankiewicz, who was 43, in 1972. The two traveled around the country together as friends, but slowly the friendship went sour. Spenkelink later said Szymankiewicz stole some of his money. In any event, Spenkelink and Szymankiewicz were sharing a hotel room in Tallahassee on February 4, 1973. That day, according to the prosecution, Spenkelink picked up a hitchhiker named Frank A. Brumm. Brumm and Spenkelink returned to the motel room while Szymankiewicz was asleep, the prosecutor said; then, without warning, Spenkelink shot Szymankiewicz in the back of the head and struck his skull with a heavy object, killing him.

Spenkelink, however, maintained that Szymankiewicz had been attacking him and that he himself had acted in self-defense. But the jury didn't believe him. On November 28, 1973, Spenkelink was convicted of first-degree murder. Brumm, who had also been charged with first-degree murder but who hadn't taken the stand during the trial, was acquitted. On December 20, 1973, based on the jury's advisory opinion, Judge John Rudd sentenced Spenkelink to death.

Spenkelink, a slender man with a shock of gray running through the center of his wavy, dark hair, had a long criminal history, including two felony convictions and an escape from a California jail. But did he deserve to die? His lawyer, David Kendall, certainly didn't think so. He felt that there were enough holes in the case to warrant at the very least a reduced sentence—and, in fact, the prosecution itself had been prepared to accept a plea bargain for second-degree murder—so he appealed to the first appellate level and then to the Florida Supreme Court, but the sentence was upheld. Those appeals took several years, and four years after the murder, Florida governor Reuben Askew finally signed Spenkelink's death warrant.

That didn't deter Kendall, however. He knew the courts offered the only chance of saving his client from death. Having gone through all the courts at the state level, he filed a new appeal in federal court. Such an appeal is called a writ of habeas corpus or a habeas corpus petition. In such a petition, a prisoner argues that his trial violated the Constitution in some way. In Spenkelink's case, Kendall argued that prejudice still guided death penalty verdicts, therefore making them unconstitutional. Even though Spenkelink was white, Kendall argued that the race of the victim could also unfairly affect a verdict. Citing statistical evidence, Kendall said that those who killed white people, such as Spenkelink, were significantly more likely to be sentenced to die than those who killed blacks. That meant that the death penalty was based on racism, Kendall argued, and that the problems outlined in the *Furman* decision had not been corrected.

At the same time, Kendall began another appeal back in Florida Supreme Court, arguing that Florida law was faulty because it had blocked Spenkelink from presenting certain mitigating circumstances that might have led the jury to be more merciful. Florida's attorney

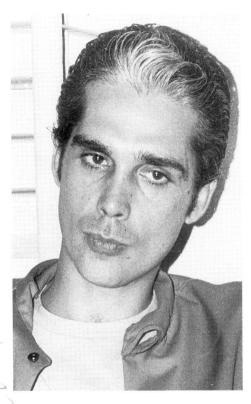

John Arthur Spenkelink. At age 19 he was charged with six armed robberies. At age 24 he killed his friend Joseph Szymankiewicz, a killing he claimed was in self-defense.

John Spenkelink's mother, Lois, and his brother-in-law, Tim Myer, at a prayer service in front of the governor's mansion in Florida. Mrs. Spenkelink had hoped to speak to Governor Bob Graham about granting her son clemency, but the governor refused to see her.

general, however, argued that Spenkelink had had ample opportunity to present mitigating facts, and the state judges agreed.

On the federal level, Spenkelink's case made it to the Fifth Circuit Court of Appeals, which in August of 1978 upheld the death sentence. The case then went before the U.S. Supreme Court, but on March 2, 1979, the Court announced that it would not hear the case.

A few weeks later, Kendall stood before a clemency panel, pleading for mercy. The clemency panel consisted of Florida's new governor, Bob Graham, and his six elected cabinet members. It was the panel's job to review the case of every prisoner on death row and decide whether or not his or her life should be spared. Every governor in the country has the power to grant clemency. If clemency is granted, the prisoner is not executed but must serve a life term.

Kendall conceded to the panel that Spenkelink had led a less-than-exemplary life. He was raised in a poor home without a father, and his mother had trouble controlling him, Kendall said. At age 19, he was charged with six armed robberies that took place in a three-hour period. But now, 10 years later, Spenkelink was a vastly different person, Kendall told the panel. Kendall read several testimonials from prison officials about Spenkelink's good behavior as an inmate. "He wasn't abusive or back-talking," Kendall explained, as he provided examples of Spenkelink's decent conduct. "He broke up fights. He helped cool down younger inmates. He read to inmates who were illiterate. . . . He ministered to a defendant in the cell next to him who had sickle-cell anemia."

Anthony Guarisco, the chief prosecutor at the trial, represented the opposing view. He detailed Spenkelink's past crimes, calling him "a career criminal," and he described Szymankiewicz's murder in graphic detail. "He has shown no signs of rehabilitation," Guarisco said, "[and] John Arthur Spenkelink is not entitled to clemency."

A month later, Governor Graham signed a new death warrant.

ON DETERRENCE

The gallows has long been the penalty of murder, and yet we scarcely open a newspaper, that does not relate a new case of that crime.

—**Abraham Lincoln,**
   16th president of the United States

If fear of death is, indeed, a fact, another fact is that such fear, however great it might be, has never sufficed to quell human passions. . . . For capital punishment to be really intimidating, human nature would have to be different; it would have to be as stable and serene as the law itself.

—**Albert Camus,**
   French writer and philosopher

The reason for expecting more deterrence [from capital punishment as opposed to life imprisonment] lies in the greater severity, the terrifying effect inherent in finality. Since it seems more important to spare victims than to spare murderers, the burden of proving that the greater severity inherent in irrevocability adds nothing to deterrence lies on those who oppose capital punishment.

—**Ernest van den Haag,**
   philosophy professor, New York University

By this time, one might think that Kendall would have given up. But he went back to the very same courts that had rejected him and tried again. Such an approach is typical of how a lawyer defends a client on death row, according to journalist David von Drehle, who wrote about Spenkelink's case in his book *Among the Lowest of the Dead: The Culture of Death Row:*

> This is the way a good death penalty defense lawyer works: . . . Go to the state supreme court, to the federal district court, the federal appeals court, the Supreme Court of the United States. Fight an issue on broad terms, and if you lose, fight it again on narrow terms. Turn every stone, poke into every mushy spot in the law. Read every opinion rendered by every court, and when some other death row inmate wins his case, shoehorn his issue into your own client's appeal. Make the law do what it promises. Make it be perfect.

Five days before Spenkelink's scheduled execution, the guards at Florida State Prison began special preparations. They had to choose the execution squad—those who would escort Spenkelink to the electric chair, strap him in, and witness the execution. They also had to test the chair and make sure the electrical generator was working. In the coming days, they measured Spenkelink for the new suit in which he would be buried, and, using a fellow guard as a stand-in for Spenkelink, they rehearsed the actual execution.

Spenkelink had already been moved to an isolation cell just a few steps from the execution chamber. All his possessions were left outside the cell, so that whenever he needed something, a guard had to bring it to him. One reason for this was that prison officials didn't want him to have anything in his cell with which he might hurt himself.

On the eve of the scheduled execution, protestors gathered across from the prison. They sang folk songs and shouted chants like "Death row must go! Death row must go!" Proponents of the death penalty had also gathered. They sat in a mobile home with a silver coffin affixed to its top and a sign urging "Go, Sparky," which was the nickname some people used to refer to Florida's electric chair. Spenkelink's mother, Lois, a 67-year-old invalid, went before the news media at a press conference and pleaded for Governor Graham to spare her child. "He won't even talk to my son," she said. "He doesn't even know my son. How can he kill my son, my only son?"

At around 8:00 P.M., Spenkelink, wearing green prison pants, the yellow T-shirt given to death-row inmates, and shower shoes, visited with his mother to say good-bye. Following that, a priest sat down with Spenkelink to keep him company during the long cold hours of the night leading up to his 7:00 A.M. execution.

At the same time, a team of top-notch lawyers was scrambling to put together a last-minute appeal. The team was headed by Millard Farmer, a leading death penalty opponent. Earlier in the day, the New Orleans Circuit Court of Appeals had rejected an appeal from Spenkelink, but Farmer hoped to convince one of the judges to issue a stay in the middle of the night, thus halting the execution, at least temporarily. He enlisted the aid of other top lawyers, including former U.S. attorney general Ramsey Clark. Clark, who had flown to Florida to join the protestors outside the state prison, readily agreed to help Farmer.

Clark called one of the judges, Elbert Tuttle. At Clark's urging, Tuttle agreed to meet with the lawyers at 10:00 P.M. in his home in suburban Atlanta. Farmer and Clark argued that Spenkelink had been inadequately represented at trial and during his appeals. They also made the case once again that the death penalty was tainted by prejudice. Tuttle agreed that things were proceeding too hastily and that the full court should once again review Spenkelink's case. So he issued a stay, and—at the very last moment—the execution was called off.

Opposing views on the eve of the Spenkelink execution. Above: A death penalty advocate has affixed a coffin and a banner that reads "Go, Sparky" (the nickname for Florida's electric chair) to his recreational vehicle. Opposite page: Opponents of the death penalty equate capital punishment with government-sponsored murder.

In Washington, D.C., similar arguments were being made. A group of lawyers from the NAACP Legal Defense Fund had rushed an appeal before U.S. Supreme Court justice Thurgood Marshall, who believed the death penalty was unconstitutional under any and all circumstances. He, too, signed a stay of execution.

Spenkelink was smoking a cigarette and watching Johnny Carson on television when he got the good news. "Thank God," he said, as the words sank in—he would live another day.

Spenkelink's relief was short lived, however. The state of Florida pleaded before both the Supreme Court and the Fifth Circuit Court of Appeals to vacate the stays of execution. Florida's attorney general, Jim Smith, said Spenkelink's lawyers had no legitimate ground for appeal. Rather, he said, they were trying to undermine the entire death penalty process. "The opponents of capital punishment," Smith told the

Supreme Court, "through questionable manipulations of the legal process, will be able to do indirectly that which they have been unable to do directly either in the state legislatures or the courts of this land."

The Supreme Court found Smith's arguments persuasive. Within two days, the full Supreme Court dissolved Marshall's stay. Justice William Rehnquist was particularly opposed to Marshall's action. Of Spenkelink, Rehnquist said: "He has had not only one day in court, he has had many, many days in court." Later that afternoon, three judges from the Fifth Circuit Court of Appeals met to consider Tuttle's stay. They apparently felt hurried because the death warrant signed by Governor Graham expired in less than a day, so instead of holding a hearing in person on the issue, they held an impromptu hearing on the telephone. It was held so quickly that neither the defense nor the state was fully

prepared. But just before midnight, the panel reached its verdict: Tuttle's stay was null and void.

The next day, on May 25, 1979, with only hours before the scheduled execution, Spenkelink's lawyers sought once again to obtain another stay—from the Florida Supreme Court and the U.S. Supreme Court. Once again the stays were denied. The execution would go forward.

A priest sat outside Spenkelink's cell the entire night. "He was smoking constantly," the priest later recalled. "He would get up, walk around the cell, then sit back down on the mattress. He vacillated between anger and trying to understand. The anger was classic convict stuff: 'These bastards can't do nothing to me.' It was obvious he was scared."

"There was a lot of quiet time," the priest added. "Every now and then, John would look at me and blow out some smoke and shake his head and say, 'In America, they just don't kill people like this.' I don't think he ever came to grips with it." At sunrise, the priest served communion to Spenkelink.

Spenkelink declined to order a last meal, but steak and eggs were brought to his cell anyway at about 8:00 A.M. The steak was already cut into tiny pieces because no knives were allowed in the cell. A short while later, guards shaved the places on his body where the electrodes would be attached—his head and his right leg. Spenkelink was then given a shower and a pair of shorts, pants, a shirt, and socks. A white paste that enhances the flow of electricity was rubbed onto his head.

At 10:05 A.M., Spenkelink was escorted to the electric chair, a large, heavy oak piece of equipment in the center of a small, white room. Guards quickly tied him to the chair with leather straps. One strap went over Spenkelink's mouth and chin to keep his head firmly in place. When he was tied down, a guard opened the blinds on a window beyond which sat a room full of witnesses.

The warden, Dave Brierton, asked Spenkelink, "Do you have any last words?"

Spenkelink responded, "I can't talk."

Some people later said Spenkelink was too nervous to talk, but others speculated that the strap over his mouth was interfering with his speech, and he would have said more had the strap been loosened. The strap, however, was not loosened, and a black leather mask was placed over his face.

The executioner, his identity concealed by a black hood, turned on the power at 10:12 A.M. A surge of 2,500 volts of electricity flowed into Spenkelink's body. Spenkelink jerked in the chair. His hands curled into fists. After a minute, the power was turned off and a doctor listened to his chest with a stethoscope. Spenkelink was still alive, so the power was turned on once again. Spenkelink survived that surge of electricity too. Finally, the power was turned on for a third time. "This time, his leg was burning. No flames, but a lot of smoke," a witness recalled. When the doctor examined Spenkelink again at 10:18 A.M., he nodded slowly to tell everyone present that yes, this time John Spenkelink was dead.

THE ARGUMENTS FOR AND AGAINST

6.

Three-quarters of the states (38 out of 50) have death penalty laws, and surveys over the years have shown consistent high support for the death penalty. In April of 1996, for instance, 79 percent of respondents to a Gallup Organization poll favored the death penalty for people convicted of murder, although an earlier poll showed that support for the death penalty dropped to 50 percent when people were offered life imprisonment without parole as an alternative.

Feelings run strong on both sides of the issue. A politician's stand on the death penalty is often an important part of his or her platform. Executions are

This crowd gathered outside the Stateville Prison in Joliet, Illinois, on August 12, 1990, to show support for the imminent execution of convicted murderer Charles Walker. The signs reflect two of the major arguments for capital punishment: that justice cannot be done without retribution and that keeping an irredeemable murderer alive costs too much money.

almost always accompanied by protests and counter-protests. Numerous books have been written about the subject, and in recent years Hollywood has joined the fray with such films as _Dead Man Walking_ (based on the anti-death-penalty book of the same name by Sister Helen Prejean).

The arguments for and against the death penalty are many. What follows is a review of some of the more prominent issues.

RETRIBUTION

Certain crimes are so vicious, so heinous that they produce an almost universal revulsion and moral outrage. These crimes may include premeditated murder, the murder of a child, or murder in which the victim is put through extreme suffering. In the face of crimes such as these, some people believe, it is appropriate—indeed necessary—for society to express its outrage by seeking retribution, by punishing the perpetrator in the most severe way possible. And that way, of course, is to kill him or her. Some supporters of this position claim a religious justification, citing the "eye for an eye" passage in the Bible. Others say that if society doesn't exact retribution for the most heinous crimes, then we really don't put much value on human life.

Opponents of the retribution argument—many of whom also begin from a Judeo-Christian perspective—see it another way. Is killing a person, even a convicted murderer, really an expression of how much society values human life? Doesn't religious tradition also call for compassion and forgiveness? If killing is wrong, they say, then it is wrong under all circumstances. As Amnesty International, which monitors human rights violations around the world, puts it, "An execution cannot be used to condemn killing: It is killing."

The retribution argument really comes down to personal morality. Charles L. Black, a professor at Yale Law, calls it "one of those ultimate clashes of value which cannot be resolved by argument."

DETERRENCE

One of the most frequently stated reasons for supporting the death penalty is the belief that it deters potential murderers from committing the crime. Some-

"Innocent persons have been executed . . . and will continue to be executed," Justice Harry Blackmun (above) wrote in 1994 in explaining why he could no longer support the death penalty.

Isidore Zimmerman (pictured here) came within two hours of execution for a murder he did not commit. Citing instances like this, death penalty opponents claim that the danger of a terrible and irrevocable mistake makes capital punishment intolerable.

one contemplating murder may be willing to risk a jail term, the argument goes, but faced with the ultimate punishment—the loss of his or her own life—the person may decide that the crime isn't worth the risk. Capital punishment may also function as an unconscious deterrent, proponents argue. By having a death penalty, society sends out a message that murder is so unacceptable that it is punishable by the ultimate sanction; this is a message we all absorb, so that intuitively, without thinking about it, we understand that we should avoid committing murder at all costs.

In 1975 an economist named Isaac Erhlich published a study purporting to show the deterrent value of the death penalty. From 1932 to 1970, Erhlich said, homicides increased while executions declined. Using mathematical formulas, he concluded that each additional execution during that time might have resulted in seven or eight fewer murders. The study was much criticized, however, because it failed to consider a wide range of factors in the murder rate, such as the rising availability of guns and the rate of migration between rural and urban areas.

Opponents of the death penalty generally reject the deterrence theory. For deterrence to work, they say, the would-be killer must think through the crime to the end and contemplate the possible punishment. And yet many murders take place in the heat of the moment, and the killer is so emotionally overwrought that he or she doesn't think about the possibility of getting caught or being executed. Even when a potential murderer does consider the possible punishment, so many obstacles stand in the way of a death sentence that few people are likely to view execution as a probable outcome, deterrence critics argue. First the murderer must be caught, then brought to trial, then found guilty, then sentenced to die. And then, of course, legal appeals must be exhausted before the execution can actually be carried out. With more than 20,000 homicides each year and considerably fewer than 100 executions, is it realistic to believe that the death penalty deters?

Additionally, some deterrence critics say, why wouldn't a lesser sentence, such as life in prison without parole, deter just as well? Stephen Nathanson, a professor at Northeastern University in Boston, argues this point when he writes: "For most of us, the prospect of life imprisonment (or even five or ten years in prison) is so dreadful that increasing the penalty for murder from life imprisonment to death would not provide any additional discouragement."

Those who argue against the deterrence theory often cite a 1980 study by two U.S. researchers who claimed that in New York from 1907 to 1963, there were on average two more homicides in the month following an execution. The researchers suggested that this might be due to a "brutalizing" effect the executions had on the populace. In addition, some observers have noted that while Texas has executed more people than any other state, its homicide rate remains among the nation's highest.

It is very difficult, however, to isolate and explain all the factors that can lead to a rise or fall in the murder rate. Few experts today claim that anyone has adequately proved empirically (with numbers) that the death penalty works or does not work as a deterrent.

COST

Cost often comes up when the death penalty is mentioned. Those in favor of the death penalty say the government shouldn't waste its money on guarding, feeding, and housing a depraved criminal for the rest of his or her life. The truth is, however, that it costs much more to put a prisoner to death than to keep a prisoner in jail. In 1995 the *Economist* magazine cited several studies pointing to the higher cost of execution. One study indicated that the cost of trying, convicting, and sentencing a killer to death, plus keeping him on death row for 8 years, is $2 million to $3 million, which is the same amount it costs to keep three prisoners in a maximum-security prison for 40 years.

Proponents of the death penalty admit that the process is costly. But they say the lengthy appeals process is partly to blame. They've been pushing hard in recent years for something called "habeas corpus reform," which will reduce the amount of time between sentencing and the execution date. (This will be discussed in more detail in the following chapter.)

POSSIBILITY OF EXECUTING THE INNOCENT

One of the most emotional arguments against the death penalty is that some innocent people have been executed, or have come close to being executed. Opponents of capital punishment say that the taking of even a single innocent life by the state makes the death penalty intolerable; better that the worst sentence be life in prison without parole so that in the event innocence is proven later, the prisoner can be set free.

How many innocent people have been on death row? That is a matter of considerable debate. A recent study by the NAACP Legal Defense Fund claims that 48 people have been released after serving time on death row since 1973. In many cases, new DNA evidence spurred the release of these prisoners.

Evidence from one state that justice isn't color-blind.

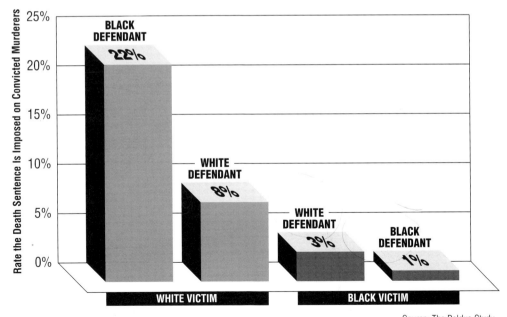

RACE AND THE DEATH PENALTY IN GEORGIA

Rate the Death Sentence Is Imposed on Convicted Murderers

BLACK DEFENDANT 22%
WHITE DEFENDANT 8%
WHITE DEFENDANT 3%
BLACK DEFENDANT 1%

WHITE VICTIM   BLACK VICTIM

Source: The Baldus Study

The most well-known review of the matter was a 1987 study by Tufts University professor Hugo Adam Bedau and University of Florida professor Michael L. Radelet. Their study, published in the *Stanford Law Review*, named 350 people who they claimed had probably been wrongly convicted of potentially capital crimes between 1900 and 1987. Most were eventually pardoned (which means the governor or president dropped the convictions and set them free) or had their convictions overturned in court because of new evidence. But Bedau and Radelet said that 23 innocent people were executed. This study was one of the reasons that Supreme Court justice Harry Blackmun decided in 1994 that he would no longer support the death penalty. "Innocent persons have been executed . . . and will continue to be executed under our death-penalty scheme," Blackmun wrote.

The Bedau-Radelet study came under fire a year later in a 1988 article, also published in the *Stanford Law Review*, by Stephen J. Markman and Paul G. Cassell, who worked in the U.S. Justice Department under President Ronald Reagan. They examined all 23 cases of people who were allegedly killed in error and concluded that there was no conclusive evidence pointing to their innocence. They accused Bedau and Radelet of relying on shaky evidence and discounting "the considered judgment of the juries and judges who decided and reviewed the cases." Still, Markman, in a later article, conceded that errors can occur. "One cannot state categorically that mistakes never have been made," Markman wrote. But Americans who support the death penalty know this already, Markman said, and yet they continue to support the death penalty "because through a combination of deterrence, incapacitation and the imposition of just punishment, the death penalty serves to protect a vastly greater number of innocent lives than are likely to be lost through its erroneous application."

RACISM

Opponents of the death penalty have long argued that racism plays a pivotal role in the selection of the condemned. This is a tradition that extends back to slaveholding times, according to Watt Espy, director of the Capital Punishment Research Project. "In the states of Virginia, Alabama and Louisiana blacks account for 85 percent of all executions through history. In the other slave holding states, the percentages

Is the application of America's death penalty racist, and if so, is that grounds for ending capital punishment? According to the Baldus Study, a comprehensive examination of capital murder cases in Georgia, a black convicted of murdering a white has a 22 percent chance of being sentenced to die, whereas a white convicted of murdering a black has only a 3 percent chance. While accepting the study's findings as valid, the Supreme Court ruled in McCleskey v. Kemp *that a pattern of discrimination is irrelevant to a particular instance.*

run over 60 percent," Espy said in a 1988 interview.

It isn't just the defendant who is sometimes singled out because of his race. The race of the victim can also play a role—and, in fact, may be the single most accurate predictor of who gets the death penalty. Two of the most authoritative studies on the issue were presented to the Supreme Court in 1987 in the case of *McCleskey v. Kemp.* McCleskey and accomplices robbed a furniture store and killed a police officer who responded to the scene. McCleskey's attorneys, who included one of Furman's lawyers, Anthony Amsterdam, wondered why McCleskey was the only person sentenced to death among 17 people charged with killing police officers in the same Georgia county from 1973 to 1980. Could it have something to do with the fact that McCleskey was black and his victim was white, they wondered?

Among the evidence submitted to the Supreme Court were a pair of studies by David Baldus, a professor at the University of Iowa, and several colleagues. The studies, generally referred to as the Baldus Study, found that if a white person was killed in Georgia, the murderer was much more likely to face the death penalty than if a black person was killed. Specifically, Baldus found that when all nonracial variables are taken into account, white-victim cases are almost 4.3 times more likely to produce a death sentence than are black-victim cases. When the races of both assailant and victim are considered, these are the rates at which the death sentence is imposed: black defendant/white victim, 22

ON DETERMINING WHO GETS THE DEATH PENALTY

How do you figure out why lightning strikes one defendant and not another? . . . [I]t's not a rational process. . . . A key factor is what kind of attorney you can afford, so the death penalty is most commonly imposed on poor people. That often correlates with people who are poorly educated, or people of color; but the issue is really less about race or class than whether they have the resources to pay lawyer fees.

—Victor Streib, professor of law, Cleveland State University

It is tempting to pretend that minorities on death row share a fate in no way connected to our own. . . . Such an illusion is ultimately corrosive, for . . . the way in which we choose those who will die reveals the depth of moral commitment among the living.

—William J. Brennan, Jr., Supreme Court justice

If blacks shoot whites, whites want revenge and capital punishment. But if black shoots black, no one cares.

—Jesse Jackson, civil rights leader and politician

percent; white defendant/white victim, 8 percent; black defendant/black victim, 1 percent; white defendant/black victim, 3 percent.

Although the Supreme Court accepted the Baldus Study's findings as valid, a 5-4 Court majority said that McCleskey had to prove that bias was involved in his specific case, and that a study presenting a pattern of discrimination was irrelevant to a particular instance. The majority conceded that "there is, of course, some risk of racial prejudice influencing a jury's decision" but felt that previous Court decisions had put in place safeguards to protect the rights of every defendant.

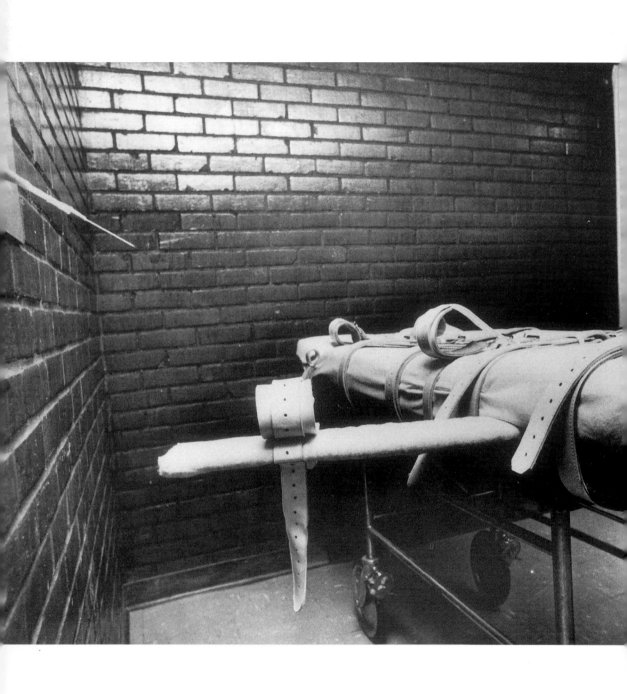

7

THE FUTURE OF CAPITAL PUNISHMENT

Of the tens of thousands of people convicted each year of violent crimes, only a couple hundred are sentenced to die, and of those on death row, only about 1 to 2 percent are executed each year. Thus, very few death sentences, in the end, are carried out. And yet a majority of the American public strongly favors the death penalty.

Historian Hugo Adam Bedau has hypothesized that Americans actually like the idea of the death penalty more than they like actual executions. He noted in 1982 that over 2,000 death sentences had been overturned on constitutional grounds since 1967 with little public outcry.

Among the world's industrialized democracies, the United States stands virtually alone in maintaining capital punishment. Pictured here is the death chamber at the Huntsville, Texas, prison. The needle protruding from the wall at left carries the lethal-injection chemicals into the condemned's arm.

The average person seems convinced the death penalty is an important legal threat, abstractly desirable as part of society's permanent bulwark against crime, but . . . he or she is relatively indifferent to whether a given convict is executed on a given date as scheduled, or is indeed ever executed.

Many other countries have been moving away from the use of the death penalty. According to Amnesty International, 47 percent of the world's nations by 1993 had either abolished capital punishment or stopped using it. Among Western democracies, the United States stands alone in keeping the death penalty. Great Britain hasn't had the death penalty since 1972. Canada abolished it in 1976. (Both Great Britain and Canada, however, retained capital punishment for excep-

Visible in the monitor at right, Roger Coleman, scheduled to die in Virginia's electric chair the following day, answers a question from talk-show host Phil Donahue, May 19, 1992. Coleman's mother, Mary Huislander, is at left. What kind of publicity an execution should receive is a matter of some debate.

tional crimes such as those committed under military law.) France followed suit in 1981. Ireland abolished capital punishment in 1990. Angola and Switzerland eliminated it in 1992, and Greece and Gambia banned it in 1993.

Over the same period, the United States has restricted its application. Most of the restrictions have come from the Supreme Court, which has heard a number of major death penalty cases over the last 20 years. Here are just a sampling of the Court's decisions: in 1976 the Court ruled that mandatory death sentences were unconstitutional; in two 1977 cases—*Everheart v. Georgia* and *Coker v. Georgia*—a Court divided 5-4 decided that the death penalty for rape and kidnapping was an excessive punishment and therefore unconstitu-

ON LEGAL SAFEGUARDS

You now have what I call "super due process" built into the [legal] system that makes it harder to get a death penalty. All the laws have safeguards built in, and in some cases, I think, [they] go overboard in making it tough for prosecutors to get capital punishment.

—**Paul D. Kamenar, executive legal director, Washington Legal Foundation**

This Court may not disregard the Constitution because an appeal . . . has been made on the eve of execution. We must be deaf to all suggestions that a valid appeal to the Constitution, even by a guilty man, comes too late. . . .

—**John M. Harlan, Supreme Court justice**

The Court . . . has recognized that the qualitative difference of death from all other punishments requires a correspondingly greater degree of scrutiny of the capital sentencing determination.

—**Sandra Day O'Connor, Supreme Court justice**

One does not need to know anything about habeas corpus *to know that when it takes 10 years or more to carry out a death sentence, something is terribly wrong with the system.*

—**Orrin G. Hatch, U.S. senator**

tional; in 1988 the Court ruled in *Thompson v. Oklahoma* that those 15 and younger could not be executed; in *Ford v. Wainwright* in 1986, the Court ruled 7-2 that executing someone found to be insane is unconstitutional. However, three years later, in *Penry v. Lynaugh*, the Court ruled it permissible to execute a mentally retarded convict. Writing for the majority, Justice Sandra Day O'Connor found that there was no "national consensus against executing mentally retarded people." Since then, however, a consensus has begun to develop. By the mid-1990s, 10 states had passed laws barring execution of the mentally retarded, as had Congress for federal crimes.

In general, Congress has stood firmly behind the death penalty. A 1994 anticrime bill approved the death penalty for dozens of federal crimes, such as treason, espionage, killing the president, genocide, causing death through a train wreck, and lethal drive-by shootings.

Congress also approved a law in 1996 limiting the lengthy appeals process that has extended a prisoner's stay on death row to an average of eight years. The law made it difficult, for instance, for a prisoner to appeal his conviction more than once to the federal courts. (The legislators had in mind cases like John Spenkelink's, in which appeals were brought before the Supreme Court five times.) Many prisoners have challenged the new law as unconstitutional, and the Supreme Court has yet to make a clear finding on it.

Some observers speculate that if the law stays in place, executions may become more frequent. If that is the case, the capital punishment debate will likely become more heated. Opponents of the death penalty think, ironically, that more frequent executions may cause a shift in public opinion and strengthen their cause. Some have even called for televising executions in order to more graphically advertise what they feel is the horror and cruelty of an execution. But there is unlikely to be any dramatic shift in the near future.

As we have seen, the death penalty has a long history. For thousands of years it remained an unquestioned tool of monarchs, judges, and governments. Only in the last 200 years has its use been called into question. Opponents of capital punishment have enjoyed their greatest successes this century, putting into place limits on the death penalty or outright bans. Perhaps one day, capital punishment will be abolished completely. But most likely, if the past offers any clue, a consensus will be hard to reach, and the debate will continue for many years to come.

Further Reading

Bedau, Hugo Adam. *The Courts, the Constitution, and Capital Punishment*. Lexington, Mass.: Lexington Books, 1977.

Bedau, Hugo Adam, ed. *The Death Penalty in America*. 3rd ed. New York: Oxford University Press, 1982.

Berns, Walter. *For Capital Punishment: Crime and the Morality of the Death Penalty*. New York, Basic Books, 1979.

Black, Charles L., Jr. *Capital Punishment: The Inevitability of Caprice and Mistake*. New York: W. W. Norton & Co., 1974.

Camus, Albert. "Reflections on the Guillotine," in *Resistance, Rebellion, and Death*. Tr. by Justin O'Brien. New York: Vintage Books, 1974.

Cohen, Bernard L. *Law Without Order: Capital Punishment and the Liberals*. New Rochelle, N.Y.: Arlington House, 1970.

Draper, Thomas, ed. *Capital Punishment*. New York: H. W. Wilson, 1985.

Flanders, Stephen A., ed. *Capital Punishment*. New York: Facts on File, 1990.

Herda, D. J. *Furman v. Georgia: The Death Penalty Case*. Hillside, N.J.: Enslow Publishers, 1994.

McCafferty, James A., ed. *Capital Punishment*. Chicago: Aldine-Atherton, 1972.

Prejean, Sister Helen. *Dead Man Walking*. New York: Vintage Books, 1993.

Radelet, Michael L., ed. *Facing the Death Penalty: Essays on a Cruel and Unusual Punishment*. Philadelphia: Temple University Press, 1989.

Radelet, Michael L., Hugo Adam Bedau, and Constance E. Putnam. *In Spite of Innocence: Erroneous Convictions in Capital Cases*. Boston: Northeastern University Press, 1992.

Trombley, Stephen. *The Execution Protocol: Inside America's Capital Punishment Industry*. New York: Crown Publishers, 1992.

von Drehle, David. *Among the Lowest of the Dead: The Culture of Death Row*. New York: Ballantine Books, 1995.

White, Welsh S. *The Death Penalty in the Nineties: An Examination of the Modern System of Capital Punishment*. Ann Arbor: University of Michigan Press, 1991.

Index

Picture Credits

Every effort has been made to contact the copyright owners of photographs and illustrations used in this book. In the event that the holder of a copyright has not heard from us, he or she should contact Chelsea House Publishers.

page

2:	Corbis-Bettmann	
14-15:	AP/Wide World Photos	
17:	UPI/Corbis-Bettmann	
20:	Corbis-Bettmann	
22:	Art Resource	
25:	The Bettmann Archive	
26:	Library of Congress, #17246	
30:	The Bettmann Archive	
31:	AP/Wide World Photos	
34-35:	UPI/Bettmann	

37:	Corbis-Bettmann
38:	AP/Wide World Photos
41:	UPI/Bettmann Newsphotos
44:	Corbis-Bettmann
47:	AP/Wide World Photos
50:	UPI/Corbis-Bettmann
53:	UPI/Corbis-Bettmann
54:	AP/Wide World Photos
58:	AP/Wide World Photos
59:	AP/Wide World Photos

62-63:	UPI/Bettmann
65:	UPI/Bettmann
66:	UPI/Bettmann
69:	Illustration by Sandra L. Taccone
71:	AP/Wide World Photos
74-75:	AP/Wide World Photos
76-77:	Reuters/Bettmann
Cover photo:	AP/Wide World Photos

ROBERT V. WOLF is a writer and editor living in New York City.

AUSTIN SARAT is William Nelson Cromwell Professor of Jurisprudence and Political Science at Amherst College, where he also chairs the Department of Law, Jurisprudence and Social Thought. Professor Sarat is the author or editor of 23 books and numerous scholarly articles. Among his books are *Law's Violence*, *Sitting in Judgment: Sentencing the White Collar Criminal*, and *Justice and Injustice in Law and Legal Theory*. He has received many academic awards and held several prestigious fellowships. He is President of the Law & Society Association and Chair of the Working Group on Law, Culture and the Humanities. In addition, he is a nationally recognized teacher and educator whose teaching has been featured in the *New York Times*, on the *Today* show, and on National Public Radio's *Fresh Air*.